MW00885182

Snippets from the Inside-Out
by Millie the Dog

Making the world a better place, one person at a time, from the inside-out!

Miss Millie's guide to self-mastery for kids of all ages

With Maryann Roefaro
Illustrated by T.B. Hill

Snippets from the Inside-Out by Millie the Dog

Making the world a better place, one person at a time, from the inside-out!

Miss Millie's guide to self-mastery for kids of all ages

Printed in the United States of America

ISBN-13: 978-1-941768-72-3 print edition
ISBN-13: 978-1-939116-25-3 ebook edition

Waterside Productions
2055 Oxford Ave
Cardiff, CA 92007

www.waterside.com

Written by Maryann Roefaro

Illustrated by T.B. Hill

Cover and layout design by Ken Fraser | ImpactBookDesigns.com

Waterside Productions

For Casey and Angela
with immeasurable love.

Welcome to Miss Millie's Snippets from the Inside-Out. Life's most significant journey is the journey people make from the inside-out. I'm here to help! I'm Millie and I'm a miniature poodle who loves every facet of life. We dogs are good at remembering things that people of all ages, shapes and sizes forget. This is partly because we love unconditionally. We love unconditionally because we know we are made from love and that unconditional love is a state of being, not an act of doing. That just means that when you know you are love, everything you do comes from that place of love. It makes for a happy life because even when life throws you lemons, you figure out some way to make lemonade!

Did you know that every relationship we have begins with the relationship we have with ourselves? That means, if you love yourself, you'll be able to love others. The more you love yourself, the more your capacity to love is enriched. The more you love yourself, the more easily you will see the good in others. The more easily you see the good in others, the nicer you become. It's really important to be nice. Practice being nice, every day. Know that everyone is only limited by the boundaries they place on themselves. You can do anything if you believe and know you can! Allow the love in your heart to spread love all over the world, one person at a time, from the inside-out.

The world is a beautiful place if you make it a habit to always look for the good in people and all situations. We all have similarities and differences and that's what makes the world precious and interesting. We are similar in that we are all made from love and love is the reason that we are on earth. We should try to **BE LOVE** every chance we can! When you are confused, ask yourself what love would do or how love would answer your question.

All our feelings and emotions are rooted or start from two basic paths – one is love and the other is fear. You can always tell the difference because love feels good and fear does not. Test it out! Think of someone you love or something that makes you happy and pay attention to how thinking that makes you feel inside your body. Now think of something that you don't like or a situation that made you angry. Notice how different that feels and how anger doesn't feel good inside. Try your hardest to always come from a place of love. If you do your best every day, your best will always be good enough!

We are all gifts to the world. Let the light that shines from our hearts fill the planet with love, joy and hope. Be the peace and love you want to see in the world. Have faith that we were made by a loving creator. Give love and you will receive it … be love and you will make the world a better place, one person at a time, from the inside-out!

Like the beauty in nature, we all need sunshine and rain to grow. For us, sunshine represents all the great stuff we celebrate and rain represents all the challenges we have actually experienced that make us stronger, smarter and wiser. Everyone has sunshine and rain in their life. Nobody escapes challenges and heartbreaks. It is important to find the opportunity in every challenge. We will never know how much sunshine or rain blesses a life, so it's better to never **judge** another but to accept the differences that make the world such a vibrant and diverse planet. Allow those who feel differently, sad or lonely to feel your love. Remember the times when you were new to a group or felt out of place or uncomfortable. Treat others the way you want to be treated and always welcome new friends and points of view into your life.

It is an extraordinary person who can experience a challenge and use all the tools they have inside to overcome difficulties. If something seems too big to handle, break it up into smaller, more manageable pieces. Always ask for help if you need it – that's one reason there are so many people on earth, especially those that love and care about you. It's important to realize that there is a reason for everything. Embrace change and challenge with love. Allow your love to make the world a better place, one person at a time, from the inside-out!

This is a refrigerator. Aren't they wonderful? They keep all our foods and drinks cold and fresh. They also keep our ice-cream frozen! Do you think about your refrigerator often or send gratitude to the universe for providing such abundance? Most people think having a refrigerator is no big deal ... until the power is off for awhile and everyone gets worried their food will spoil. Don't wait until the power goes off to appreciate your refrigerator or anything else in life. It's important to appreciate all life's gifts, all of the time. People are most important and it's important to tell the people you love that you love them! Try your best not to go to sleep angry or mad at somebody. You'll sleep better if you slumber in love.

Always be grateful. **Gratitude** is one of the keys to a happy life. Feel and show appreciation in all that you do. Don't take any of life's gifts for granted. Everything on our planet is on loan to love and enjoy while we live on earth. Treat everything like a gift that you appreciate and cherish.

Start out every day giving thanks for everything you have and end every day giving thanks for all that you've received. Don't wait until the power goes out to appreciate anything. Allow your gratitude to flood the world, and make it a better place, one person at a time, from the inside-out!

This is a picture of one rope. The rope is made by tons of fibers or threads that are woven together to make it one rope. A rope is very strong because of the sum or total of its parts; many threads but one rope. Life is like this. Many people yet one planet; many planets yet one universe.

Notice the end of the rope – some of the individual fibers are showing. Those fibers are not very strong alone. It takes the whole bunch of fibers working together to lift or hold heavy objects. Partners, families, teams and communities are all examples of how people working together can get more accomplished than working alone. When there is a lot of work to do, many hands make the job much less difficult or stressful. Don't be afraid to reach out for help when you need it. A real friend will always be available with a helping hand when you need it. Knowing that we are all connected and part of the oneness of life gives us a more **global perspective** to love and respect everyone and everything in the world.

Family, friends, communities, states, countries and continents working together are stronger than any can be alone. Fill your world with love and gratitude. Together, know that you are part of those strong fibers that make everything around us stronger! Let your love of humanity help unite the world from the inside-out!

This is a glass of water. Is it half full or half empty? Only you can decide. Life is like this. Everyone makes a decision every day to look at the glass as half full or half empty. If you see the glass as half full, you see positivity and potential. You see the value of the contents and show gratitude for its existence. If you see the glass as half empty, you are making a decision to focus on "lack or have not" instead of "have." Only you can make the choice whether to see what you have and be happy for it – or to see what you don't have and be unhappy that you may be missing out on something.

Perception is how people look at things and interpret or understand them. A person's perceptions make things real to them. Sometimes people make things appear real or act like they are real, but they are not. People make them real because they believe they are real, but sometimes they don't have all of the information or there has been a misunderstanding or miscommunication. Can you think of when this has happened to you?

Your outlook and attitude about life determines if you look at this glass as half full or half empty. Try to look at life as though the glass is always half full –full of love, gifts, opportunity and celebrations. Think positive in all that you do. Make the world a better place, through your positive and loving outlook on life, starting from the inside –out!

This is a grocery or shopping cart. They are fun to ride in if you are little like me! You can tell a lot about a person from how they treat a grocery cart.

Grocery carts are provided by stores. The stores are generous because they provide them to all their shoppers. The workers take good care of them and make sure they are available when needed. People should be accountable when they use them and always be considerate of others. They should be grateful for the use of these temporary gifts. They should keep them safe and clean and always return them to the proper locations when they are done using them. They should respect the property and kindness of the cart's owners. Life is like this.

Be accountable for all you think and do. Take responsibility for your actions. Be honest and never be afraid to admit a mistake or admit that you don't know the answer to something. Nobody has the answers to everything! Honesty and integrity are characteristics that build good families, businesses, and communities. Make an effort to never bully anyone. Always be kind and considerate. Don't take anything for granted – even the little things like shopping carts that make life easier. Be kind, loving and grateful in all that you do. It will make the world a better place, one person at a time, from the inside-out!

Have you ever seen a graph? This is a picture of a graph. There is one vertical axis and one horizontal axis. The horizontal axis is the line that goes from left to right and represents the good times and tough times in life. The good times are easy days when life is full of fun and happiness. The tough times are when life has struggles like high stress situations, sickness, loss of someone or something very special, events that cause distress, etc.

The vertical axis is the line that goes up and down and represents personal growth. The curved line in the middle is opportunity or the journey of self-mastery. It's a never ending journey because it has no end or destination. Each day, we have opportunities to learn things about ourselves and love ourselves and others more. Notice that personal or inside growth is highest during the toughest times.

If we understand that there is a reason for everything, we can try to figure out what we are supposed to learn from all our experiences. Notice the word extraordinary in the body of the graph. It's the tough times in life that help us build resilience. **Resilience** is one of the keys to a happy life. Resilience is the stuff inside that helps us believe that we can overcome obstacles. Resilience is the part of the power within that gives us great strength and courage to move forward even in the most difficult situations to make ourselves and the world a better place.

This is a picture of me with some of my friends. They are very different from me but I love all of them. It's wonderful for me to communicate with different kinds of animals. They each have their own special perspective and I can learn so much from them. No matter where they live, it's always so much fun to bump into them.

Birds can really tell you a lot about the world. They have such a global view of things, being able to fly. They will often tell me how small even all my human friends look when they are flying high – we can learn something from this. Sometimes when a challenge seems too big for us to handle, it's important to step away from it. The farther away you can get, the smaller the challenge will appear. As your perspective changes, and you give it some time, when you go back to the challenge it often looks different. Sometimes putting a bit of time and distance between you and the challenge really helps you figure things out and resolve the stuff that bothers you.

Get excited about the differences that all living things bring to the world. Don't be afraid of humans that are different from you. Be **tolerant** of all people and know that everyone has their strengths and weaknesses. Sometimes those strengths and weaknesses are on the inside and sometimes they are on the outside. No matter what, be the tolerance you want to see in the world by being love.

Glasses can be fun! Even though not everyone goes around wearing glasses, they still see the world through their own personalized lens. This lens is created by all their experiences and by how they think and react to all the events life can offer. This is why five people can look at one thing and see it or interpret what they're looking at five different ways. Everyone sees things a little bit differently and can bring forth different ideas and creativity to situations.

I like magnifying glasses, too. They make small things look much bigger. They are very helpful when you want to see something close up that is very small. People's minds can magnify issues and that is not always helpful. When a person focuses on something, it gets bigger and it can appear overwhelming. A little problem can become a big problem just by thinking and believing it's a big problem. Sometimes it's helpful to take a step back, outline the issue in writing and make as list of possible solutions. If the issue seems really big, break it down into smaller parts to make it easier to think about and solve.

You may hear people talk about power. **Power** does not come from how big somebody is or how old they are or how much money or things they have or by their job. Power comes from love and it comes from within. Love yourself more every day and be the peace and joy you want to see in the world!

Remember that every relationship we have begins with the one we have with ourselves. When we love ourselves, we will love others. When we always see the good within ourselves, we will easily and readily see the good in others.

When we give love freely, it will come back to us in even greater quantities than we gave it. If you want more love in your life, love others more. If you want more laughter in your life, laugh more!

When we are nice to ourselves and forgive ourselves for not being perfect, we will be nice to others and we will forgive others for not being perfect. This will allow us to not place our expectations on others and set us and them up for disappointment.

As you think about yourself and life, pay attention to the words you use to talk to yourself. Are you being mean to yourself or kind to yourself? Always be kind to yourself – the more you use nice words to talk to yourself, the more resilient and strong you will become.

Respect yourself and others. Share your talents with those who can use your help and always try to be of service to those who have less. Allow the love in your heart to make the world a better place, one person at a time, from the inside-out!

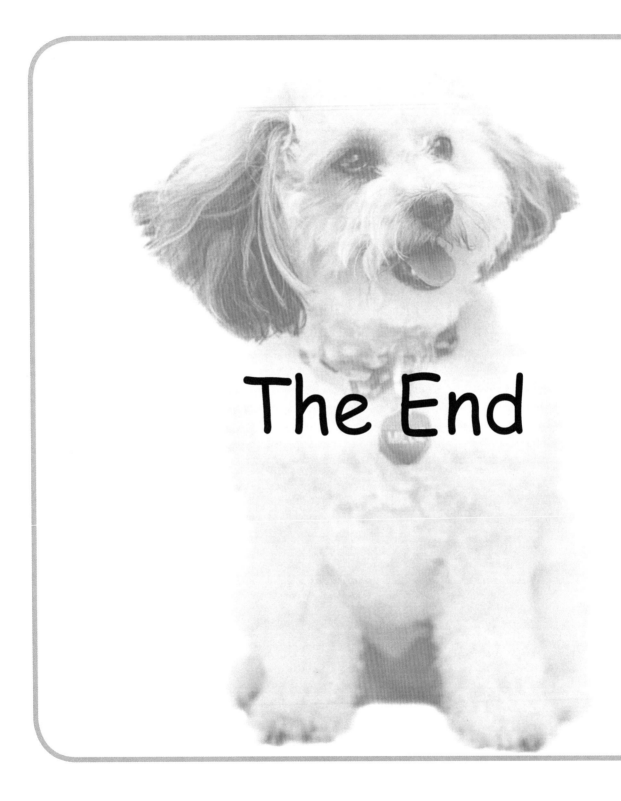

The End

About the Author

Maryann Roefaro is a highly intuitive spiritual mentor. Dedicating her career to healthcare, she has over 30 years of executive leadership experience. She has been the CEO of the largest private cancer practice in Central New York, Hematology-Oncology Associates, since 2002. Author of "Building the Team from the Inside-Out" and "A Human's Purpose by Millie the Dog," she maintains an active role in leadership and spiritual development through various speaking engagements and internet radio shows.

Maryann received her Doctor of Divinity from the American Institute of Holistic Theology, her MS Degree from Upstate Medical University, and her BS from Albany College of Pharmacy. She is an ordained minister through Metaphysical Universal Ministries. She is a Certified Heart Centered Hypnotherapist and a Reiki Master Teacher. She is also a certified ChiRunning and ChiWalking instructor.

Maryann is married to Tom Carranti and has two daughters, Casey Angela Prietti and Angela Marie Franz and two step-sons, Pio Peter Carranti and Joseph H. Carranti. Millie is her adorable miniature poodle with a sweet disposition and a beautiful heart and soul. Mare, Tommie and Millie live in Central New York.

Made in United States
North Haven, CT
23 March 2024

50386123R00018